AN OPEN LETTER FROM WRITER / PRODUCER VICTOR PISANO

Dear Educator:

Every film project begins with high hopes and expectations. Many end up falling short, however, either in the eyes of those involved in the making of the film or those who view it. I feel extremely gratified then, that THREE SOVEREIGNS FOR SARAH came as close as it did in reaching the hearts and minds of almost everyone who worked on it or has viewed it. Our files are filled with letters of inquiry and support from such far-ranging sources as a fifth-grade class outside of Washington D.C., a Bible study group in Vancouver, a graduate law class at an Ivy League university, to genealogists from all over the country. In light of this, composing a useful Teacher's Guide became an interesting challenge in its own right.

The series takes place during one of the shortest transitional periods in American colonial history - the late 1600's. It was a period where every aspect of day-to-day life was in flux. Clothing styles, for instance, were becoming more expressive and less rigid. People had begun to "survive" the onslaught of winter - they had "dug in." A paradox really, because there was also an undercurrent of uncertainty and insecurity. As Sarah herself describes, the King of England had been overthrown. The government of the Province of Massachusetts, what there was of it, was weak and waiting for a new charter. In the midst of all of this, church leaders of the colony complained of "backsliding" religious values, and Indian attacks were a constant threat. Compounding this problem was the fact that the only familiar boundary the Puritan colonists looked out upon was an expanse of treacherous ocean facing a home continent which in a real sense had banished them to begin with. On the opposite side, they confronted an endless series of hills - an almost impenetrable wilderness with no known limits, inhabited by savages and wild beasts. This was the environment and atmosphere of the Province of Massachusetts in 1692.

When I set out to put together a production team, I had in mind to assemble a group of talented visionaries who could have survived the harshest trials of the period themselves - production is often hell. For instance, there were only a few articles of clothing left of the period - anywhere. Our Costume Designer took the bull by the horns and researched the intrinsic designs, construction methods, and materials. The resulting wardrobes that she brought to the production numbered almost one hundred separate articles of clothing made not only to the exact specifications of the period, but were constructed of the original materials as well, such as, handwoven linen, cotton, and wool.

Upon completion of the production, the costumes were donated to the Essex Institute Museum of History in Salem to safe-keep as the only complete replication of men and women's clothing of the period.

In similar "fashion," I instructed the Art Director to be prepared to turn the sound off of the finished film and simply "experience" the look and feel of the late 1600's. The result was an authentic visual feast of the period, from rare "line-back" cows to distinct architecture and household items. In fact, some of the "props" were not really props at all, but 300-year-old artifacts from Salem Village archeological digs.

The production team on this project was possessed in their own tasks, if you would pardon the expression. Add the support of a gifted cast and crew and a moving story, and we were well on our way to success.

THREE SOVEREIGNS FOR SARAH is unique in many ways. First, there exists no other production for cinema, television or stage that comes as close to the historical accuracy and integrity as this movie portrayal. Second, the in-depth story is powerfully conveyed by three Academy Award winners in the lead roles; Vanessa Redgrave as Sarah Cloyce, Kim, Hunter as Mary Easty and Phyllis Thaxter as Rebecca Nurse. It was our intention that something new be revealed each time the series was viewed. This Teacher's Guide will assist in isolating those key points of interest. In this way, we will be able to allow you to collect those points relative to your area of interest or study on as many levels as the series encompasses.

- ABOUT CREATIVE LICENSE -

By nature, every historic dramatic production or "docudrama" has to take some creative license, and THREE SOVEREIGNS FOR SARAH is no different. Only, it wasn't necessary for us to take many liberties with our production because the actual story was already powerful and dramatic. The old adage, "truth is stranger than fiction" holds water here. I decided early on that if we were going to embellish the story, it would be in a way that could have happened or at the very least would not have been out of place in context. The few creative licenses that were taken, were used as a "vehicle" to move the story along.

Taking scant or incomplete historical facts and building an authentic story around them takes pragmatic insight as well as a creative instinct. Our three preeminent historical advisors, Professor Stephen Nissenbaum, period specialist, Peter Cook from Plimoth Plantation, and Salem Village Archivist Richard Trask, were all kept busy referencing and cross-referencing dramatic content. Needless-to-say, there were some few points of contention, even among experts on subtle interpretive elements. But this is the true value in the study of history or historical events. History is not just a long series of chronological dates strung out in line. It lends itself to interpretation and opinion. It's this quality that makes human history most relevant for study. Even history-ln-the-making with all it's television and newsprint coverage draws a tremendous divergence of opinion. Sunday mornings are full of television shows loaded down with panels of "experts and journalists" who never seem to agree on well-covered events of the day let alone obscure incidents buried in 300-years of history. THREE SOVEREIGNS FOR SARAH should be viewed as a historical account in this light.

Specifically, THREE SOVEREIGNS FOR SARAH takes its largest creative license in the way the story is told when Sarah appears before the three Royal Magistrates. There was no such review process for Sarah to take her appeal. The three sovereigns were used as a creative "device" accordingly. Also, the story is told through the eyes of an accused person, Sarah Cloyce, and therefore has a decided bias toward the victims of the hysteria. I'm sure Sarah herself, however, would have agreed with the way this story is portrayed. The Reverend Mister Samuel Parris, on the other hand, would have undoubtedly favored another version. Such is the telling of history. The series is presented in an accurate albeit subjective, way but includes an extensive bibliography for comparative study. We like Sarah's version and believe It will hold up best against time.

With regards to characterizations. When the script for THREE SOVEREIGNS FOR SARAH was first researched, only a handful of people, most of them historians, actually knew who the main characters were. Virtually no one knew about the leading character, Sarah Cloyce. Sarah was one of three sisters accused of witchcraft and the only one of the three not to be hanged. This is the cornerstone of this true story. As portrayed, after her release from jail, Sarah spent what little time she had left in life in the pursuit of clearing her sister's name. In real life, she died thinking that she had failed. When Sarah Cloyce's story was resurrected in script form, perhaps one hundred or so people knew of her or read her story. During the production phase of the project, a thousand or more learned of her. But after the first night airing on PBS national television, 15 million people knew of Sarah, her sisters, and their story. Finally, with the release through PBS Video, the mini-series will continue for generations to come as a teaching tool to additional untold numbers. Ultimately Sarah did clear the names of her two sisters Mary and Rebecca - they were exonerated on a grand scale, just as her character promised she would do... "If it should take me an eternity."

www.Salem-Witch-Trials.com

(NOTE: We created this TEACHER'S GUIDE with large text and plenty of column and paragraph spacing for tutorial notes and additional questions by the instructor.)

THE SALEM WITCH HYSTERIA
(A CHRONOLOGY AND BACKGROUND)

by Richard B. Trask

(Mr. Trask, the town archivist of Danvers, Massachusetts, formerly Salem Village, served as a historical advisor on "THREE SOVEREIGNS FOR SARAH." He is recognized as one of the leading authorities on the subject today. In 1970, Mr. Trask lead a historical dig which located and unearthed the famed parsonage house of The Reverend Mister Samuel Parris. Artifacts of household items found at the site were painstakingly recreated and used as props during the entire filming. Some of the movie props were not props at all, but relics from this dig. Here are Mr. Trask's views on the subject.)

There are few footnotes in American history which have been more read about and been the subject for more theories than the famous witchcraft outbreak in Salem, Massachusetts. Writers and scholars, down through the decades, have tried to explain these events as being the result of religious backsliding in New England, the pranks of bored adolescents, the influence of the oligarchical and power-hungry clergy, mental aberrations, spiritualist goings-on, political and cultural tremors, clinical hysteria, economic backlash and even ingested fungi.

The fascination of the 1692 Salem witchcraft hysteria simply will not die, largely because the subject of witchcraft conjures up intriguing theories among the public. The witchcraft cases are also extensive enough to represent a diversity of people and events, yet manageable enough to be studied in microcosm.

The ordinary English Puritan settler in New England during the 17th century believed, as did his European counterpart, in the existence of the devil and the possibility or witchcraft affecting his everyday life. Witches were believed to be humans who had agreed to serve the devil, obtaining certain amazing powers in return from the devil, and who attempted to bring ruin upon the Christian community.

On continental Europe, beginning in the 15th century, literally thousands of "witches" had been discovered and put to death. Due to certain cultural and religious differences, witchcraft outbreaks in England had been less dramatic, yet up through the 17th Century an estimated 1,000 "witches" had been hanged, usually during periods following social or political strife.

The English settlers of New England did, on occasion, find witchcraft at work within their various communities, and although a large scale witch outbreak did not occur prior to 1692, some 90 individual cases are documented before that date.

One of the larger Massachusetts Bay Colony settlements was Salem, first settled by Europeans in 1628. Some five miles west of Salem center was Salem Village (now called Danvers), an agrarian area politically a part of Salem Town but which beginning in 1672 was able to tax itself for support of their own minister. Many of the approximately 500 inhabitants of the Village desired full independence from the Town, and due to internal problems arising from controversies over their ministers, as well as social and economic differences among the villagers, the area had acquired a reputation of provincialism and ill-feeling.

In 1689, a former unsuccessful merchant of the West Indies named Samuel Parris became the fourth minister of Salem Village since 1672. Instead of his coming being a quieting influence, his settlement spawned continued problems over his salary and status.

During the bleak mid-winter of 1691-92, Elizabeth Parris and Abigail Williams, the minister's nine-year-old daughter, and eleven-year old niece began exhibiting wild and unusual behavior. Shouting, falling into apparent trances, attempting to run into burning fireplaces, and having terrible fits and convulsions, the girls quickly aroused the concern of their family and neighbors.

As time passed, instead of improving, the girls' symptoms began to spread among others in the Village. The fits were not playful antics to those who witnessed them. They were obviously real and frightening. The village doctor, William Griggs, had no explanation for the grievous illness, except to conclude that the evil hand was on them. Fasts and prayer sessions were conducted by Reverend Parris and neighboring ministers but to no avail.

Just why did the girls experience these fits? Scores of later writers have offered their opinions, but the original records provide scant direct evidence. It does appear, however, that Tituba, Reverend Parris' Carib Indian slave, had been telling the girls of the household, and later other impressionable young girls, vivid stories of fortune telling, witchcraft and other forbidden topics of the day. After much suffering and upon the continued insistence of their elders, the "afflicted children" named three women whose specters, invisible to all but the girls, were supposedly tormenting them.

These three accused "witches," who included Tituba herself, were examined by local magistrates at Salem Village on March 1st, 1692, and held over for trial. But the frenzy over witches did not end with these women being jailed. More and more people, men and children as well as women, were also accused, and a number of them confessed to being witches.

For the next half year, fear spread all over Essex County and the Massachusetts Bay Colony as over 150 suspected witches from numerous communities were discovered, examined, and jailed. Following the establishment of a special court to try the accused, 19 persons were found guilty and hanged, while one man, Giles Cory, who would not plead his case, was tortured to do so, and died under the weight of stones placed upon his body. Besides those victims who were executed, at least three others of the accused perished in jail, succumbing to terrible living conditions and ill-health.

Not everyone, however, was under the sway of hysteria, and as opinions of other clergy and authorities were finally sought and considered, the witchcraft proceedings and accusations abated. By October of 1692, the Governor of Massachusetts declared a jail delivery of those imprisoned, and the courts no longer allowed to convict persons on such one-sided and tenuous proof as spectral evidence, which had been accepted earlier in the year.

For years following, the stigma of the witchcraft hysteria remained. Salem Village became independent from Salem Town in the 1750's, and its name was changed to "Danvers." With the passage of time, and with the realization that it had been a period of human frailty, historians and scholars were able to look at the Salem witchcraft hysteria in another light. Although it had been an infamous period, the events also produced genuine heroes - people who saw the hysteria for what it really was and who risked death to stand up for the truth.

**Richard Trask town historian and archivist of Danvers, MA
(Salem Village)**

THREE SOVEREIGNS FOR SARAH

- VOLUME ONE -

(48 minutes)

(52 minutes with credits)

THREE SOVEREIGNS FOR SARAH, the three-part, three-hour special presentation in the humanities mini-series about the Salem Witch Trials begins in 1703 with the appearance by Sarah Cloyce (Vanessa Redgrave) before a Royal Court of Inquiry called into session in Boston to examine the events surrounding the Salem Witch Trials which took place in Salem Township eleven years previously.

Sarah, who was accused of practicing witchcraft in 1692, spent more than one year in jail before being released. She appears before the Chief Magistrate (Patrick McGoohan) to try to clear her name as well as the names and reputations of her two sisters - Rebecca Nurse (Phyllis Thaxter) and Mary Easty (Kim Hunter). Both of Sarah's sisters had been hanged as witches during the witch hysteria that gripped Salem Township over a fifteen-month period in 1692-93.

Sarah begins her testimony by recalling the atmosphere in Salem Village in 1689 as the village inhabitants became involved in a hotly contested dispute to select a new minister. When Samuel Parris, an unsuccessful and former merchant of the West Indies is chosen as the new minister, his selection does little to calm down the ill-will among neighbors that exists in the village.

If anything, the bad feelings grow even worse as feuding village elders argue over the new reverend's salary and status. It's clear by Sarah's testimony, that she was on the anti-Parris side of the dispute.

In a flashback sequence, a weak and infirmed Sarah relates the events as they unfolded. During the bleak mid-winter of 1691-92, several young girls in the community began to act strangely - shouting, going into trances and experiencing trembling fits and convulsions. Among them are Reverend Parris' nine-year-old daughter Elizabeth, and his eleven-year old niece Abigail Williams. They were influenced by mystical tales and conjuring of the West Indies told them by their household slave, Tituba, as a diversion against boredom.

The village doctor, William Griggs, unable to attribute the symptoms to any known disease, concludes that the children have been attacked by some kind of "evil hand." Hunger fasts and prayer sessions are held but do not relieve the situation.

Finally, at the prodding of some of the girl's elders, including Reverend Parris himself, the "afflicted children" soon begin to name names of the "specters" who were tormenting them. The girls claim that are they being afflicted by the specters of three women in the village. Although no one else can see these specters, the three women are nevertheless arrested, jailed, and charged with the practice of witchcraft. Among the arrested is Reverend Parris' slave, Tituba.

Soon, the accusations begin to spread throughout Salem Village. Sarah tells of how innocent women, men, and children are arrested on spectral evidence alone, each being accused of witchcraft and sent to jail.

Episode One ends in the Spring of 1692 with the arrest of Rebecca Nurse, Sarah's oldest sister and a God-fearing woman who had been regarded as a pillar of the community. Although Rebecca proclaims her innocence, the elderly woman is arrested in the sickbed of her bedchamber and charged with the practice of witchcraft.

Rebecca Nurse stands accused of witchcraft in Salem Village.

THREE SOVEREIGNS FOR SARAH

- VOLUME TWO -

(49 minutes)

(52 minutes with credits)

Episode Two of THREE SOVEREIGNS FOR SARAH begins In the Spring of 1692 just after Rebecca Nurse, Sarah's oldest sister, has been arrested and charged with the practice of witchcraft. This is the true beginning of the hysteria, for, before this time, only women of lowly rank and position in the community were accused of such practices. When Rebecca is brought before the two Magistrates In the village meetinghouse, it constitutes a new turn of events. Here was a known reputable soul. If Rebecca Nurse was brought before the Judges, then no one was beyond suspect or the reach of the accusing girls. (This opening sequence uses the actual transcripts of the hearing).

Rebecca continually responds that she cannot possibly be under the devil's influence and that she is as *"clear as the child unborn."* The meetinghouse is filled with villagers and inquisitive onlookers from all over the area. Rebecca's piety appears to sway even the most suspicious. But, just as she seems to be convincing the Magistrates, some of the "afflicted children," seated in the front, suddenly go into convulsions and point to Rebecca's unseen specter which they claim bites and pinches them. The most curious of those who appear to be tormented, is an adult, Anne Putnam, the mother of one of the girls. Sarah relates in this part of the story that Anne Putnam (Sr.), was one of the original Reverend Parris supporters siding against Sarah and both of her sister's families. The court clerk during the entire melee is none other than the Reverend Mister Samuel Parris himself.

When questioned if the devil appears in her shape to torment others, Rebecca half responds in a confused state, being that she was hard of hearing. This confusion is final proof for the two Magistrates that there is evidence enough for Rebecca to be jailed and to be formally charged with the crime of witchcraft. This divides Salem Village into even more defined lines - one side rising in power, one side in retreat. Sarah does not retreat, however. She dismisses the possibility that she herself could stand accused if she came to her sister's defense. Sarah chooses to fight. She attends the next service conducted by Reverend Parris only to have him quote scripture saying that just as Christ was betrayed by the devil, the devil was likewise amongst good Christians in Salem Village in the shape of other Villagers. Sarah sees this as a slanderous power grab by Parris and storms out of the meetinghouse slamming the meetinghouse door behind her to the screams of newly tormented children.

Sarah continues to tell her story to the Special Royal Court in 1703. She recounts that she was then arrested on the charge of witchcraft as she expected she would be. Sarah's hearing soon follows - a trial of will and faith ensues between Sarah and the Reverend Samuel Parris. But Sarah welcomes the confrontation, resolved that her faith in God would prevail. Sarah is nonetheless forced to join Rebecca in Salem Jail as one of the accused. The accusatory girls now become more confident after Sarah's imprisonment. Other townships soon employ the girls of Salem Village to ferret out witches within their own communities.

Episode Two comes to an end when the last and most pious sister of all, Mary Easty, is accused of witchcraft by the afflicted children. She is arrested in her garden and taken away by the village Sheriff.

Sarah challenges Reverend Samuel Parris in the Meetinghouse

THREE SOVEREIGNS FOR SARAH

- VOLUME THREE -

(49 minutes)

(52 minutes with credits)

As Episode III of THREE SOVEREIGNS FOR SARAH begins, Sarah Cloyce continues her narrative of the Salem Witch Trials for the Special Court of Inquiry sent by Queen Anne of England to Boston to determine the facts surrounding the nine-month witchcraft hysteria which took control of Salem Village eleven years earlier.

She picks up her story in the summer of 1692 when she and her two sisters, Rebecca Nurse and Mary Easty, are in prison together having been arrested and charged with the practice of witchcraft.

Following her trial, in which she was found guilty, Rebecca is excommunicated from her covenant church and hanged with four others also found guilty of practicing witchcraft. Soon after, Mary Easty has her trial and is also found guilty. She is hanged for her "crime," but not before delivering one of the most eloquent pleas for sanity, not in her own defense, *"but that no other innocent blood be shed."*

By this time, nineteen people had been tried and hanged, and one old man, Giles Corey, was pressed to death for not entering a plea at his own trial. Salem jail is now jammed with more than 100 other accused persons awaiting examinations and trials, including the minister who was fired from Salem Village prior to Reverend Parris' arrival.

As a result of this overcrowding, some of the accused are moved to private homes where they are incarcerated. Sarah herself is transferred into the custody of one such private jailer, a farmer, in the neighboring town of Ipswich where she remains for more than one year awaiting her own trial. Sarah is convinced throughout her stay in the farmer's jail that she will follow the fate of her two sisters to the hanging tree.

By this time, a high-ranking Council of Ministers finally recommended to colonial government officials decreeing that "spectral evidence" alone should no longer be accepted as the sole factor of determining guilt or innocence for people accused of witchcraft. This was the factor which virtually ended in its tracks all witch trial proceedings in Salem Towne. Pinching and biting by unseen spirits could no longer be proof of guilt for witchcraft. When no other evidence is provided, it all collapses. So the hysteria stopped here.

As a result of this decision, all of the accused people in jail are ordered released, once they paid their court and prison costs. Though innocent, they were still obligated to pay those costs. When Sarah is finally released from her own incarceration, a little more than one year from the time of her arrest, she begins a grueling crusade to prove the innocence of herself and her two sisters.

The crusade culminates in 1703 when the Special Royal Court of Inquiry assembled in Boston listens to Sarah's testimony and finds that she and her sisters have indeed been wronged. The Third Episode concludes when the Chief Magistrate presents Sarah with three gold sovereigns as symbolic compensation for the miscarriage of justice brought upon them in 1692 - one gold sovereign for the sovereignty of each sister's life.

Sarah died three weeks later.

Chief Magistrate reviews the case of Sarah Cloyce

- PONTS OF INTEREST -

The "Points of Interest" section of the Teacher's Guide is designed to assist the instructor or the history buff by pointing out specific areas that might be of interest to those who view the production. These points are nondenominational in scope, meaning they may cover a variety of fields of study and interests. Primarily, however, these points will be of a historic nature, relating particularly to the fabric of the work and to its authenticity. Obviously, this section should be used after the series has been viewed at least once completely through uninterrupted.

The Points of Interest section has three columns. The First column is under the heading: "TIME into Episode." Below that is the notation, "(min./sec.)." This column is meant to be used in conjunction with your VCR, television, computer or other electronic video viewing equipment. All viewing devices have FREEZE FRAME capabilities in one form or another. Some have running times as well. Use this column to calibrate the Points of Interest. As a last measure, an iPhone stopwatch will work just as well.

For example, if the First column notation reads; "15 / 43," it simply means that the particular Points of Interest to be observed is 15 minutes and 43 seconds into the Episode. A FREEZE FRAME stoppage within one or two seconds either way of this notation will suffice in almost every instance. It is important, however, to remember to set the minute/second counter to "00:00" at the beginning of each Episode at the first frame of picture video.

The Second column will give a brief description of what is being isolated and what to look for in that scene.

The Third column on the right, if applicable, will raise the related question(s) regarding the Points of Interest. Have fun…

Points of Interest

(Volume One)

Time into Episode (min. / sec.)	Description of Point	Questions Raised
00 / 15	The two-wheel cart was the primary utility cart used by farmers of the Period. Four wheel wagons were not in widespread use until the middle of the 18th century.	*Was this two-wheeled cart unique for the 1690's?*
02 / 53	In the 1600's, main front doors of dwellings often reflected the status and wealth of the man who owned the building. If there was a studded nail pattern in the door with lots of nails, for instance, or a set of highly worked hinges, it was a declaration to others by the owner of that door that he was a man of wealth. They were a form of plumage. Nails and elaborate hinges were an expensive commodity of that era. The ability to afford extra panes of glass in windows was another consideration of a person's wealth. The larger the pane of glass and the number of them was another declaration of wealth. In the case of the door in this scene, it fronts an important government building as indicated by the color of the door and the pattern of the nail design.	*Why were there so many nails and extra fancy hinges on the front doors of some buildings?*

Time into Episode (min. / sec.)	Description of Point (Vol. One)	Questions Raised

03 / 30   Behind the three diamond-paned windows are three Royal Magistrates appointed by Queen Anne of England. There were usually at least three Magistrates present at all levels of review. Rarely if ever would one judge alone preside over cases. The numerical "three" plays an important symbolic role in this story on many levels just at it has throughout history. The ancient Greeks, for instance, referred to it as the "perfect" number in full complement and harmony to what they considered the perfect shape - the circle.

Why is the number "three" used as a symbolic number in THREE SOVEREIGNS FOR SARAH? Can you think of other significant usages of the number three in this series?

04 / 35   One of the three Royal Magistrates addresses Samuel Nurse as "Mister" Nurse as opposed to "goodman" Nurse, noting that Samuel Nurse had only recently acquired the title of "Mister." At that time, a man could not have the title of "Mister" without owning substantial property and holding a high social status within the community. Likewise, the title "Mrs." referred only to a woman who was married or widowed to a man of such acquisitions. "Goody," short for "goodwife," meant that the woman was either married or widowed to a man who had little or no property and was just of average rank or status. The term "Mr." or "Mrs." was understandably a rare moniker.

Why was Samuel Nurse allowed the honor of being addressed as "Mister" Nurse?

Why did Sarah refer to herself as "Goody" Cloyce instead of "Mrs." Cloyce??

Time into Episode (min. / sec.)	Description of Point (Vol. One)	Questions Raised
05 / 35	Notice that the three Royal Magistrates have before them a desk full of paraphernalia. Most of these tools, like the inkwells and writing implements, were original items of the early 17 hundreds while others were recreated props, accurate in every detail to the originals. The actors were confused sometimes as to which were which. The style of wigs the Magistrates wear are called "full bottom wigs." Even today, full bottom wigs continue to be used in the courts of the United Kingdom.	*The three Royal Magistrates have many different and unusual things on their desk. How might have some of them been used?*
08 / 30	This drag-style plowing technique went out of practice in the late 1600's when iron for plowshares became more readily available and blacksmiths more widespread. In this case, a heavy weight such as a pile of boulders was placed on a spiked platform. The spikes needed constant repair because they were most often made of wood. Metal was rare (remember the nails in a wealthy man's door?) Horseshoes were a prized possession as well.)	*How does this plow differ from other drawn plows? How is this design supposed to work? Why wood and which plow would work better?*
08 / 40	This small style Puritan meetinghouse was typical of the period (1650-1700). It was both a place of politics and a place of worship - the town hall and the town church were combined as one. This meetinghouse was constructed for THREE SOVEREIGNS FOR SARAH by wood shipbuilders	*How did the Meetinghouse of the period differ in style and purpose to churches of today?*

24

Time into Episode (min. / sec.)	Description of Point (Vol. One)	Questions Raised

08 / 40
(cont'd)

in Boston, using "original" Salem Village church records and witchcraft records as construction guidelines. Like the original, this meetinghouse was constructed of massive oak beams with interlocking mortise-and-tenon joints and included an open ceiling structure and stylized curved truss and buttressed supports. There are only bits and sections of other meetinghouses left of the period. The few existing remaining structures were inappropriate for shooting in because they had been modified and incorporated into other designs of other periods. There are no unencumbered buildings looking like this one-of-a-kind structure anywhere. It specifically belongs in 1692 and existed nowhere else until we built this detailed replica. Our meetinghouse was "aged" by 20 years for the production by the art department. It still stands on the Rebecca Nurse homestead in Danvers, Massachusetts, one half-mile from where the original meetinghouse stood - both faced the same easterly direction.

How did the Meetinghouse of the period differ in style and purpose to churches of today?

09 / 50

In this scene, Young Joseph Putnam is dressed in the affluent style of a man of property even though just a youth. Joseph Putnam was only 19 at the time. "Style" is an important word here, for, during this period, personal clothing had become more expressive and less

How have hair styles changed in American society in the last 300 years and why?

Time into Episode (min. / sec.)	Description of Point (Vol. One)	Questions Raised

09 / 50
(cont'd)

rigid than just a few decades earlier. What's more, long hair was also fashionable for well-to-do men because it meant, for one thing, that they were not heavily involved In manual labor. It was yet another outward reminder of one's position in life and their assumed place within the community.

How have hair styles changed in American society in the last 300 years and why?

A century or two earlier in Europe, long hair was a necessity for survival in hand-to-hand combat against sword slashes to the back of the neck. Long hair was always a sign of longevity and success - unless you were a laborer in the 1600's in America.

How was a soldier's hairstyle in the middle ages a part of his armament?

11 / 35

The wages of ministers were paid by the attending parishioners of the church. The church was made up of Puritans who wanted to "purify" the English Anglican Church and thus set out following the teachings of John Calvin. For this reason, these Puritans were sometimes referred to as "Calvinists."

Why were ministers chosen by village elders as well as church elders? What is a Calvinist?

With the meetinghouse doubling both as a place of worship and the town hall, heated debates such as this were commonplace because church elders were usually town elders as well.

What conditions and demands did Reverend Parris make before he would accept the vacant position of minister of Salem Village?

Time into Episode (min. / sec.)	Description of Point (Vol. One)	Questions Raised

11 / 35
(cont'd)

In Salem Village, the meetinghouse was the only building which belonged to the village itself. The rest of the village fell under the jurisdiction and protection of the Towne of Salem by the Sea, five miles to the east. Therefore, a volatile mixture of church and village politics ensued, creating many undercurrents and widespread ramifications.

How can one determine what a minister's status was within the community?

Reverend Samuel Parris was at the end of a line of ministers who had much difficulty dealing with factions of the village. The village had gone without a minister for more than a year and many people were becoming irascible because of it. When Samuel Parris finally accepted the position (offered by one faction of village elders) he set conditions and made several demands which had to be met by the entire village before he would consent to serving. More squabbling left things unresolved. Parris came anyway.

Was a minister's status higher or lower that the elders who offered Rev. Parris the position? Were they higher or lower than elders who did not want Rev. Parris as their minister?

Ministers of the period were always addressed as, "The Reverend Mister _ _ _ _ _ _ _ _ _." The term Mister elevated them up to the highest level of the community.

What is the status of a minister today by comparison?

Time into Episode (min. / sec.)	Description of Point (Vol. One)	Questions Raised
12 / 05	This is a surviving parsonage of the period (circa 1683), the Reverend Joseph Capen House, in the neighboring town of Topsfield, Massachusetts, the town where Sarah and her sisters grew up. This parsonage is similar in shape, size, and stature to the parsonage house occupied by the Parris family in Salem Village from 1698-1697. Even though the parsonage belonged to the village, it was status enough for all ministers to be labeled "Mister."	*When a Puritan minister was awarded a parsonage, was this considered his personal property?*
13 / 00	Tituba, variously spelled; Titabe, Titibe, Titiba, and Tituba but correctly pronounced "Tid·a·ba." Tituba was Reverend Parris' slave and was a full-blooded Carib Indian of the West Indies, not mulatto or Black as was incorrectly portrayed for the last century and in many other productions. John Indian, Tituba's "common-law" husband, was also a Carib Indian. They both came with Reverend Samuel Parris and his family as property from the West Indies.	*Were Black People the only people of color to be enslaved by the Puritans?* *How did the Puritans justify keeping slaves of any race?*
13 / 28	"Three" cords of wood, delivered by Reverend Parris' supporters, were scarcely enough for two months use by an average sized family. Wood was cut in long, four-foot sections for easier transport, stacking and measuring. A cord of firewood, then as now, is a stack of wood equal to 128 cubic feet (usually 4 ft. high, 4 ft. wide and 8 ft. long).	*How much wood did Reverend Parris demand for his services as minister of Salem Village?* *How much wood did he get?*

14 / 44

One's social position in the village was reflected in where one usually sat in the meetinghouse during religious services - men on one side, women on the other. Those paying the greatest amount or rates to the support of the minister as well as those having the highest social position, sat in front pew-boxes while lesser contributors and common folk sat toward the back according to their rank. (The more property a man possessed, the higher his contribution to the minister's salary and the closer he and his wife sat to the front of the church, each in their own separate box of gender.

In this portrayal, why were the girls of the village forced to stand in the back of the women's side of the church/meetinghouse?

By standing in back, where did this place the girls in relationship to their status in the village?

Some of those wealthy men, however, like young Joseph Putnam, opposed Parris as a choice and refused to pay anything but still sat in front because of his name, status, and inheritance. Status was blatantly exhibited. The closer you were to the front box-pew, the higher your place on the social ladder. Yet another visual reminder of where one literally stood in relationship to his or her fellow villager. Remember, these people all shared a common heritage, language, race and cultural background and were even tied by one religious belief. So, where one sat in the church was a "primary" way of visually determining status among neighbors. Climbing the social ladder was not just a figure of speech in 1692 – it was lived out.

Why are Israel Porter and Joseph Putnam sitting beside Thomas Putnam and in front of Samuel Nurse?

How does this scene relate to the way status is measured today?

15 / 30

The phrase "new holy covenant" spoken by Reverend Samuel Parris meant, essentially, a new agreement between God and the contributing members of his particular "living" church - a reaffirmation and brand new start. It signified the formation of a new congregation, headed by a new minister and most importantly, represented the likelihood of a new seating arrangement in the scheme of things.

What new changes would take place in Salem Village church once Reverend Parris formed a new covenant? What is a church covenant?

16 / 00

This is a major part of the actual first sermon given by the Reverend Samuel Parris to his congregation. This sermon was delivered as importantly as setting up constitutional town-law. Reverend Parris chose this Biblical passage for the edification of his staunch followers and benefactors in the front pew-boxes.

What was Reverend Parris referring to when he named his Text and read, "The living God is among you?"

17 / 00

Naming a Text was more like "declaring" Text in Calvinist services because it literally was the "lesson of the day."   Naming Text also appears in some of the transcripts of the trials when Abigail Williams, one of the afflicted girls, jumps up and screams out to Parris, *"Minister! Now name your Text!!!"* The naming of Text was tantamount to a commandment in the Puritan church of 1692.

For his first service, however, Parris picked Joshua: 3: 9-11.

When ministers of today "name their Text," does it carry the same ominous weight?

Time into Episode (min. / sec.)	Description of Point (Vol. One)	Questions Raised

19 / 10 — Children, especially girls, usually had hours of involved scripture lessons each day with domestic teachings and chores. There were only a few holiday observances. Christmas, Easter and Thanksgiving as we know them were not celebrated. Dancing and even bathing were not practiced either. Church services most often took up an entire day and were conducted on "Sacrament" Sunday as well as one day mid-week. Boys had a little more freedom than girls being pressed into more outdoor activities such as farm chores and hunting. Children often spent a great deal of the time thinking of their futures and who their marriage partners might be.

Why were the girls od Salem Village so easily distracted from their studies?

What household chores would be required of girls but different for boys?"

21 / 25 — Cleansing by fasting was a common practice, still observed today in many cultures and religions, it not only purged what was ingested, it sometimes led to "visions" after three or four days. Notice here that the two girls "stand" at the dinner table and do not sit. Children always stood in the presence of their parents at dinner.

Why was Elizabeth Parris forced to fast?

Why were the girls forced to stand at the family dinner table?

Time into Episode (min. / sec.)	Description of Point (Vol. One)	Questions Raised
23 / 00	Raw egg whites suspended in water give off a certain distortion of light akin to solid clear crystal which was an extremely rare item in colonial America. Egg whites served as a reasonable poor man's substitute crystal ball and were readily available to the girls because of their domestic duties. Fortune-telling was forbidden because it directly conflicted with teachings of the church. However, it was a widely held belief that these "folk beliefs" could be effective in telling the future. People of the period were highly vulnerable to superstitious beliefs, especially poor country folk.	*Why was Anne Putnam Sr. so willing to let her daughter Anne Jr., join in the fortune-telling even though it went against the teachings of the church? How do these superstitions compare with superstitions of today?*
25 / 15	Interestingly enough, the two girls living in the Parris household became "afflicted" first. They were the youngest of the group and the most influenced by Tituba's storytelling. Once the other older girls mastered the practice of fortune-telling, they often acted on their own, showing others and led by Anne Putnam Jr.	*Were the girls of Salem Village play-acting or were they really possessed?*
26 / 40	The original afflicted girls were of two households - that of Reverend Samuel Parris and the house of his chief supporters, Thomas and Anne Putnam.	*Compare the fits experienced by Bette Parris and her cousin Abigail to the fits of other afflicted girls of the village.*

Time into Episode (min. / sec.)	Description of Point (Vol. One)	Questions Raised
27 / 45	Reverend Parris and Anne Putnam Sr. indirectly (or directly) influenced and reinforced the girls with their "spells" by not discounting them as afflictions or aberrations or as fakery. Both Reverend Parris and Anne Putnam Sr. were in fact bolstered in a conviction and were naive and superstitious at the very least in handling such matters. That is, of course, if they didn't have ulterior motives in mind as Sarah believed they did.	*How did the Reverend Mr. Parris and Anne Putnam Sr. influence the early "afflictions" of the girls in their respective households?*
28 / 55	Dr. Griggs wears a small beard which was out of fashion by the late 1600's. Only a few old men wore beards as a carryover from earlier times. Dr. Griggs was a throwback physician in many respects. His examination of the two girls in the Parris household is often described as it appears here.	
31 / 21	In past accounts, Dr. Griggs used the term "Bewitched" as his diagnosis of what was afflicting the girls. The term voodoo was not a part of Puritan colonial vernacular. However, Reverend Parris, having been a merchant of the West Indies, was most likely familiar with the word "voodoo" and how it applied in this case. Thus the links to Tituba. It's quite clear and reasonable as to why the witch hysteria started inside Reverend Parris' household with his sickly and impressionable nine-year-old daughter Bette, instigated by his West Indian slave Tituba and superated out into the vulnerable village as paranoia so dictated.	*How would Dr. Griggs' examination differ from a modern exam given by doctors of today?* *Where are the West Indies and what role did they play in the slave trade?*

33

Time into Episode (min. / sec.)	Description of Point (Vol. One)	Questions Raised
34 / 00	Anne Putnam Sr. was the first adult to become "afflicted." From actual court records, these are her purported words and fits as they took place. The words were entered as evidence in later trials as a testimony against accused persons.	*Why was Anne Putnam Sr. the firs adult to be stricken with strange fits emulating the girls?*
35 / 38	This was the famous account of the meeting of local ministers led by Reverend Samuel Parris as recreated here in word and action.	
35 / 40	Notice that Dr. Griggs and the assembled ministers ask Abigail, *"What is it, child?"* Reverend Parris alone asks, *"Who do you see?"* Abigail does not offer names at this time, most probably because she knew of no one outside of the minister's influence and would not likely name one of them. Abigail was also Reverend Parris' niece and lived with him along with nine-year-old Bette Parris. Coincidentally, they were the first two girls to have fits. From this point forward, however, both of these girls received a great deal of attention from a group of the most powerful men in the area. In fact, these most powerful and influential of men dropped to their knees and began praying before both of the children who lived under Reverend Parris' roof.	*Why is Abigail Williams silent when asked, "Who do you see?"*

Time into Episode (min. / sec.)	Description of Point (Vol. One)	Questions Raised
36 / 40	The "witch-cake" was a true conjuring of "white" English folk magic, told to Tituba by a common village woman named Mary Sibley. Tituba was scared of what was happening with her diversionary afternoon games and sought help. The "water" or urine of some of the afflicted girls was mixed with rye meal, baked, and then fed to the Reverend's dog. This might have been the derivation of the ill-researched theory of "rye-mold" induced delirium. The witch hysteria simply did not happen that way. Tituba probably never heard of such a witch-cake test prior to this. This substantiates the belief that Tituba feared that things had gotten out of hand and that she was desperate and afraid of the ramifications if no answers were found. In fact, Tituba was the first "witch" to be named by the very same girls she cared for - a name supplied by her slave-master, the Reverend Mister Samuel Parris.	*Why did Tituba bake a witch-cake made of rye meal and why did she have to go to someone else in the village to learn how?*
39 / 00	This is a famous scene taken from several historical accounts where the names of the first accused witches came forth. It's the adults in the room who actually place the names of the girl's tormentors out in the open for them to consider.	*Where did the names of the first accused come from?*
39 / 14	First, Parris implicates Tituba directly, forcing the issue - then Anne Putnam Sr., the first afflicted adult, comes forth with her notorious words, *"I can think of two such women - they must be..."*	

40 / 22	One of the Royal Magistrates comments on the serious implications of accusing the girls of "lying" in naming names. Lying, in any form, was looked upon as a malicious un-Christian-like act unbefitting girls in a Christian house let alone ones who resided in a parsonage. Lying was very uncommon in a Calvinist setting. No one lied. Rebecca Nurse had been bedridden for several months with a stomach ailment. Before that time, she would often walk to her covenant church in the Town of Salem, five miles away. She attended the village church on occasion as a matter of convenience for it was visible from her farm.	*Why was it hard for the three Royal Magistrates to believe that the girls were lying as a group?* *Compare lying during Puritan times with lying of today.*
43 / 00	This long scene in Rebecca's bedchamber is documented in form and content, ending with her famous words, *"Let them come... Let them come."* What was added to the scene was the little-known fact that Anne Putnam Sr. had a special association with Rebecca and her two sisters (collectively the Towne sisters) dating way back. They all grew up in Topsfield, Massachusetts where at one time, Anne's family (the Carr family) accused Sarah and Rebecca's mother of witchcraft over a land dispute.	*Why was Rebecca Nurse willing to "let them come?"*

- END OF EPISODE ONE -

Points of Interest

(Volume Two)

Time into Episode (min. / sec.)	Description of Point (Vol. Two)	Questions Raised
00 / 28	Most of this scene was taken from the actual transcripts of Rebecca Nurse's hearing and trial. Notice that there are "three" officials present; Magistrate Judge Jonathan Corwin, Magistrate Judge John Hathorne and The Reverend Mister Samuel Parris himself. All three were assigned as "official keeper of the records" for trial. Even then, it was understood that what gets reported to history is a function and slant of those who set it to print. Reverend Parris was also known for his quick, tight handwriting ability.	*How does Anne Putnam Sr. turn the tide against Rebecca?* *How were the witch trial proceedings conducted?*
	It is purported that more than a century later, famed American novelist, Nathaniel Hawthorne, added the letter "W" to his last name because he was a direct descendant of Judge Hathorne and he wanted to separate this ignoble association by adding the extra letter.	*Was Reverend Parris the best man for the job of court clerk? Was he impartial?*
	This scene In 1692, however, speaks for itself. Notice that it's Anne (Carr) Putnam Sr., who jumps up and presses the issue when the girls initially fail to follow through on their accusations of Rebecca.	*Do you believe that every word was accurately recorded? Why?*

Time into Episode (min. / sec.)	Description of Point (Vol. Two)	Questions Raised

09 / 00

Judge Hathorne proclaims to Rebecca that she will be sent to Salem Jail, *"paying those costs yourself."* People who were incarcerated in the late 1600's had to pay for their own jail costs and expenses. They, or their family, paid for everything including food and chains. Few could afford the cost of a single cell and, were placed in a large holding cell with a number of other prisoners of both sexes. Even if a prisoner was found innocent or acquitted, they were not permitted to leave the jail until their debt was paid to the jailer.

How was the jail system of the late 1600's in the colony different from today?

10 / 10

At the end of Rebecca's hearing, the underplay of tension in the village became most evident. The immediate outcome of the hearing saw neighbors, as well as families, join in separate factions. At one point, Judge Hathorne is confronted in the middle of the hearing by his own brother-in-law, town elder Israel Porter, leader of the anti-Parris group, and begs him to stop the nonsense, *"In the name of God!"* Similarly, Young Joseph Putnam confronts his half-brother, Thomas, and Thomas's wife Anne Sr. Joseph ushers his famous threat to them in their faces, *"You will be sorry if you touch anyone in my household with your foul lies."*

Was this kind of treatment "cruel and unusual punishment – then and now?"

10 / 50

This was a well-mixed, almost incestuous group of people, each having strained associations of property, family, and entitlements. Clear sides formed through blood, church, property, status, and politics.

What was the indication that family feuds played a major role in Rebecca's sentencing?"

Time into Episode (min. / sec.)	Description of Point (Vol. Two)	Questions Raised
11 / 25	Israel Porter and his son-in-law, Joseph Putnam, were key leaders against the Reverend Samuel Parris and his supporters. Porter and young Putnam were the most powerful tandem in the village. Yet, with all their influence, they had to back down when spectral evidence was allowed as primary evidence against the accused. It was formidable opposition because there was no way to defend against it – invisible spirits attacking the bodies of children in front of everyone to "see?" It was not a precedent, because spectral evidence had been routinely accepted in English law for nearly a century prior to this date.	*What is "spectral evidence" and why was it so hard to defend against it?* *Why was spectral evidence allowed?*
	As for Samuel Nurse, he was still a "goodman" at this point and could wield little or no power without the help of Israel Porter and young Joseph Putnam. This is how the Salem Witch Trials started and who caused it.	*What part did local politics and family associations play as factors in the witch trials?*
13 / 25	Sarah makes the point that *"Their women accuse our women."* Remember the early incident Sarah alluded to in Topsfield between the Carr family and the Towne family. Also, men of property (all titled "Mister") were the only ones eligible to vote in the village meetinghouse. Once the two sides of the Parris controversy were drawn, it was the wives of the men on one side accusing the wives of the men on the other. It mushroomed to include others after that.	*What did Sarah Cloyce mean when she said, "Their women accuse our women."?*

14 / 55

This was the scene which inspired this mini-series. It is the actual account of the confrontation between goodwife Sarah Cloyce and The Reverend Mister Samuel Parris. Until this time, it was "Mr." versus "Mr." of the village, or "Mrs." versus "Mrs." Sarah, a commoner, becomes the first women to directly take on the issue of witchcraft and the minister - all by herself. Women were not only denied the vote, they were expected to keep their place. They were not allowed to address meetings or to sit with their menfolk at religious services. It must have been quite a daring feat, therefore, not to mention reckless, when Sarah defiantly stood up and questioned the minister at Sacrament Sunday. Following that defiance, Sarah storms out of the meetinghouse, slamming the door behind her to a choir of tormented girls. This known episode became the core of the mini-series. How could it not?

Why did Reverend Parris pick this specific Text from the Bible?

Why did Sarah stand?

How dangerous was it for Sarah to defy Reverend Parris in front of the congregation?

What were Reverend Parris' explanations as to why witches were attacking Salem Village?

15 / 15

Historical records tell us that Reverend Parris caused this confrontation by "naming his Text," John; 6:70, where Jesus knows he is about to be betrayed by the devil in the shape of a disciple, Judas Iscariot. "Jesus answered them, *"Have not I chosen you twelve, and one of you is a devil?"* There wasn't much subtleness in the minister's choice of Text that day nor in the words he directed at Sarah as she stood, *"The Lord Christ knows how many devils there are in his church... and who they are."*

Why did the "evil hand" single out Reverend Parris' household in his mind?

Time into Episode (min. / sec.)	Description of Point (Vol. Two)	Questions Raised

19 / 15 — Sarah knew that after her confrontation with Reverend Parris, that the minister would use his station as a man of God, leaning heavily on scripture as an attack position against those who opposed him - his last choice of Text being evidence of that. Sarah chooses the same device as her only means of defense, knowing that she would soon be accused as it was with her sister Rebecca. Wisely, Sarah's defense, Biblical Text, was a sort of reverse spectral evidence. It would be spectral evidence versus spiritual conviction. Sarah was trying to defeat spectral evidence by presenting a more powerful specter of her own - the Holy Ghost.

Why did Sarah use scripture as a defense against the minister?

What did Sarah mean when she said, "It's not they [the afflicted] that I speak to." Who is Sarah speaking to?

She starts by uttering to herself one of the Ten Commandments, *"Thou shalt not bear false witness against thy neighbor."* Her "temple of God" defense was a creative license, but not far off the mark for what was known about Sarah. Like other women of the village, she attended frequent services and concentrated Biblical study. No wonder conversations and vernacular of the day were so heavily laced with phrases and quotes from the Bible as unquestioning directives.

Why was Sarah's chosen Text from Corinthians' declaring herself to being a "Temple of God" a perfect defense?

22 / 22 — The physical "witch" examination is self-explanatory. Virtually all accused persons were so examined after their arrests. Blemishes, warts or skin anomalies of any kind, would be considered as evidence against the accused.

Why were the accused body-searched for skin defects?

Time into Episode (min. / sec.)	Description of Point (Vol. Two)	Questions Raised
23 / 23	Only a narrow account of Sarah's actual hearing survives to this day. This scene is an accurate compilation, however, of Sarah's hearing along with other hearings of many of the accused taken from original documents of the court and transcripts of the trials. The information that did come down from Sarah's hearing, enabled us to recreate the scene in temper and intensity as it most probably transpired.	
25 / 45	After Sarah declares herself innocent and presents her "temple of God" defense, no one was willing to speak up against her. Original documents, however, show that it was John Indian, Parris' man-slave, who sheepishly steps forward and accuses Sarah directly of *"pinching me and biting me, 'til the blood came."* Her response inside the meetinghouse also survives to this day.	*Why was Reverend Parris' slave, John Indian, allowed to give testimony against Sarah?*
28 / 55	The transferal of diabolic fluid from the accused back to the afflicted by a simple touch was used as a test in England on a number of occasions. It was a carryover from European witchcraft trials where thousands of "witches" were convicted and burned at the sake a Century before.	*What was "diabolic fluid" and how was it used as evidence during Witch Trials here and in Europe?*

Time into Episode (min. / sec.)	Description of Point (Vol. Two)	Questions Raised

31 / 45 Repeating the Lord's Prayer clearly, without making the slightest error or stutter was another test of guilt or innocence during the Salem Witch Trials. It is difficult enough to repeat any verse without faltering once, especially under the great pressure the accused undoubtedly felt. The version of the Lord's Prayer that Sarah repeats is from the 1611 King James' version of the Bible which was used almost exclusively by Puritans during this period; *"Our Father "which" art in heaven... "in" earth as it is in heaven... Forgive our "debts and debtors,"* and so on. Every word had to be perfect.

When Sarah flawlessly finishes her recital she asks, *"There, be you satisfied!?"* No one was willing to step forth for the longest time. No one wanted to say she had or had not repeated the Text perfectly for fear of being wrong either way in front of the entire village. Not even the judges nor Reverend Parris uttered a word for the same reason.

Try repeating clearly and out loud any well known poem, verse or prayer without slipping or pausing unnaturally.

Why did no one respond to Sarah when she asked, "There, be you satisfied?"

Which side won the confrontation between spectral evidence vs. the scripture in this instance?

34 / 30 Salem Jail was made of reinforced post and beam wood construction, very much like a barn or solid house. There were periodic escapes, however, by prisoners who simply bribed freedom from their jailer. Some speculative reports claim that the prisoners were sometimes able to just kick out the wooden side-planking and escape that way.

What would be the most likely way to escape from Salem Jail by all historical accounts?

Time into Episode (min. / sec.)	Description of Point (Vol. Two)	Questions Raised

36 / 50 — Giles Cory was a notoriously belligerent farmer and outlander of the village. He had no interest in anything the village did or the politics it was caught up in. After being accused of witchcraft, by his own disgruntled wife, Cory refused to enter a plea of either "guilty" or "innocent" as an implicit denial that the court had any right to try him at all. It was a law of the Colony that no one could have a trial without a declaration of guilt or innocence - so Cory stood mute. The court then tried to "press" either word out of him by borrowing another technique from European witch trials called "Peine Forte et Dure." This was the first and only time this form of torture by placing rocks on top of someone was ever used in North America.

The last two words Cory would plea were, *"More weight."*

Why did Giles Cory refuse to enter a plea of either guilty or innocent at his own trial?

What does "Peine Forte et Dure" mean in French?

42 / 00 — It became apparent to many of the accused that persons who confessed to being witches were, for the foreseeable future, left alone in jail while the non-confessors, considered dangerous witches still able to ply their evil powers, were first to be tried and subsequently hanged. In fact, NO accused person who confessed to being a witch was ever hanged. A reprise was worth a false confession to over 40 accused persons who thereby "belied" themselves. The 40 often had strong family pressures urging them to confess to being witches because of this fact. Understandably, many took this route to save themselves by confessing but not people of strong Calvinist beliefs. This was why many were vulnerable to accusations. They would not, or more accurately could not, confess to something that would jeopardize what they viewed as their most prized possession - their eternal soul.

Why did Tituba confess to being a witch?

Why did the accused Sarah Goode instruct her four-year-old daughter, Dorcy, to confess to being a witch?

Why did Sarah Goode not confess?

Time into Episode (min. / sec.)	Description of Point (Vol. Two)	Questions Raised

42 / 00
(cont'd)

Sarah reflects this point before the Royal Magistrates when she states, *"No true Christian would ever claim allegiance to Satan. Why would they save their lives only to lose their souls?"* The unwillingness or "inability" for Puritans to lie sealed the fate of innocent village Christians who were accused by their enemies. There was no defense.

Did some of the accused take advantage of confessing to being a witch?

Would you lie to save yourself or someone in your family?

44 / 55

When the new governor William Phipps arrived in the Province of Massachusetts, one of his first acts was not what the prisoners of Salem Jail had hoped for. They were chained. The afflicted girls claimed that by keeping the hands and feet of the accused shackled, it eased their own torments and suffering. Phipps obliged, having more pressing matters to attend to - an Indian uprising in the neighboring Province of Maine.

Why was the first edict of the new Governor of the Massachusetts Colony to chain all prisoners of Salem Jail?

Not many months later, the governor's own wife would be accused of practicing witchcraft.

- END OF EPISODE TWO -

Points of Interest

(Volume Three)

Time into Episode (min. / sec.)	Description of Point (Vol. Three)	Questions Raised
00 / 30	Mary Easty evidently was a very animated woman, especially with her hands, using them often and expressively. She was also recognized as perhaps the most pious of the sisters and one of the most irreproachable of all the accused. She was initially cleared of all charges because of her piety and grace.	*Why was Mary Easty originally found innocent?*
01 / 35	Although briefly identified in the Series, the man holding the Bible in Salem Jail is Reverend George Burroughs, one of the ministers of Salem Village prior to the Reverend Samuel Parris. Reverend Burroughs moved his family out of Salem Village to the Province of Maine shortly after a financial dispute with Thomas Putnam. Not surprisingly, Burroughs was accused of witchcraft by Parris' niece, Abigail Williams. The authorities hunted Reverend Burroughs down in Maine even during the Indian uprising and arrested him. Reverend Burroughs was placed on trial and found guilty of all charges of practicing witchcraft. Spectral evidence was the only proof along with his unusual boisterous personality and unorthodox style of preaching Text. He would eventually hang along with eighteen others. This case against Reverend Burroughs helped to coin the phrase, "witch-hunt."	*Were ministers ever accused of practicing witchcraft in 1692?* *If so, for what specific reason outside of spectral evidence would be given to accuse a minister?*

Time into Episode (min. / sec.)	Description of Point (Vol. Three)	Questions Raised
06 / 40	To a dedicated covenant member of the Puritan church, the most horrific punishment one could receive was not the death penalty, but to be cast out of the church by excommunication, a communal acknowledgment that the person was dead to the "living" church. (Remember Parris' first sermon siting, *"The living God is among you."*) Taking away Rebecca's soul in this manner left her with only an empty shell - her earthly body. The excommunication was performed at her own covenant church in Salem Towne by its minister, the Reverend Mister Nicholas Noyes.	*Why did Rebecca consider herself dead when her minister snuffed out the candle and closed the Bible in front of her?*
09 / 30	Spectators, children as well as adults, were always present at public hangings. The afflicted girls were there in full numbers as well. Those accused who were hanged were bound hand-and-foot with linen ties partly so that no specter could jump from the accused and do bodily harm on the innocent "afflicted" that had assembled to watch them hang. It was traditional practice in most other hangings as well. Those who were hanged were carried to the tops of ladders where they stood perched until they were simply pushed off - a procedure called appropriately enough, "turning off." They did not usually suffer broken necks but rather died of strangulation.	*Who attended the public hangings in 1692?*

Time into Episode (min. / sec.)	Description of Point (Vol. Three)	Questions Raised

13 / 25 All hanged persons were considered aligned with the devil, thereby having lost their immortal souls. After being cut down, the bodies were systematically dumped in open crevices or behind walls, without a burial, Christian or otherwise.

Why were the bodies of those who were hanged not buried?

15 / 50 In the still of darkness, Samuel Nurse found the body of his mother, Rebecca, and brought her back to her home in Salem Village where the family buried her in a secret unmarked grave, the exact location of which remains unknown to this day.

Why did Rebecca's son Samuel wait until dark to retrieve his mother's body?

19 / 30 Mary Easty's documented plea to the governor of Massachusetts and influential ministers of the time was one of the most eloquent documents to survive the Salem witch period. It illustrates the powerful self-sacrificing beliefs of many of the people of the day. Mary's hands, again, play an important part in this story.

Why did Mary think that the afflicted were both "possessed" and "not possessed"?

23 / 00 Even though the Parris forces had apparently assumed open domination of the village, hardly anyone was attending services held by Reverend Parris in the meetinghouse. This could have been out of fear of incrimination or simply a sign of nonsupport for the minister. Parris' salary, technically paid for by the "entire" congregation, had dwindled to almost nothing at all. This, oddly enough, was at the apex of the witch hysteria, which was by now running rampant throughout the countryside.

At the eight of the witch hysteria, why was Reverend Parris' salary nearly cut off completely ?

Time into Episode (min. / sec.)	Description of Point (Vol. Three)	Questions Raised
26 / 10	Martha Cory, one of the 19 people hanged as a witch, was actually accused of being a witch by her own husband, Giles Cory before he was himself pressed to death for not entering a plea.	*Who accused Giles Cory's wife of practicing witchcraft?*
27 / 18	Notice that the executioner allows Mary's hands to be tied in front of her as opposed to behind, as was customary. He wasn't as sure about Mary's guilt and allowed Mary her last prayers.	*Why did the executioner allow Mary's hands to be tied in front?*
29 / 20	When local jails became overcrowded, "private" jailers were allowed to use their own houses or farms to keep prisoners for a price. Remember, it was the prisoner who paid the jailer directly for their stay in jail, not the colony. Beside supplemental income, being a private jailer for the accused witches was also a way of keeping the accusatory finger away from their own doors. Jailers and their families were never accused of witchcraft. Strangely enough, because the community was so small, many of the private jailers knew their prisoners as either neighbors or friends.	*Why would anyone of that era offer their services as a private jailer?*
31 / 45	Some private jail conditions were as harsh as those in Salem Jail, while other gave their prisoners free run of the house. Sarah was not one of the fortunate prisoners. She stayed in an unprotected shed during her entire incarceration.	*Why did Sarah's private jailer refuse to speak to her or to untie her hands?*

Time into Episode (min. / sec.)	Description of Point (Vol. Three)	Questions Raised

33 / 30   Sarah's husband, Peter Cloyce, was rather ineffective during her whole ordeal. First, he was only a "goodman" and second, unlike his wife Sarah, Peter was of a school of thought that one should not, or could not, stand in resistance to accepted authority. Outwardly defying the law of the land was just not done no matter how unfair it seemed to the individual. Civil disobedience was unheard of and almost a century away in America. Hardly any of the families of the accused spoke up or defied the sentencing. At best, they would only quietly petition and acquiesce. Most, however, were like Peter, withdrawing instead into complacency - isolation and hopeless despair. They were powerless to act, or so they believed.

Why didn't Sarah's husband Peter, attempt to rescue her from her private jailer?

What recourse did the families of the accused have?

35 / 15   In his own private despair, Samuel Nurse, Rebecca's son, chops down a representative tree, not unlike the one they hanged his mother on.

36 / 46   Sarah was freed after Peter repaid her Jailer, exactly one year from the time she was arrested. Once spectral evidence was no longer allowed as sole evidence, the accusations simply stopped because there was no other proof to condemn the accused. From beginning to end, the Salem Witch hysteria ran its course in a little over a year. During that time, over 150 people were accused of witchcraft and 20 lost their lives, 19 by hanging and one being pressed to death. Several more died in jail while they were awaiting trial. The number of afflicted increased as well before it all ended in the spring of 1693. No "afflicted" person was ever hanged or incarcerated.

How long was the Salem Witch Hysteria from beginning to end?

How many people ended up accused and how many died?

Time into Episode (min. / sec.)	Description of Point (Vol. Three)	Questions Raised

40 / 30   The list of names, as well as the map, was creative license only in the respect that it was never pointed out at the time - but could have been. The meetinghouse was not only the center of the village, it was the center of the controversy. It was shared communally as both church and town hall by everyone in the village. All other influences, taxes, and political matters in Salem Village fell under the jurisdiction of Salem Towne. Those who lived closer to the Town of Salem felt its influence the most and wanted independence from it. They were also the "anti-Parris" faction as well. Those furthest away supported Salem Towne and Reverend Samuel Parris. They did not relish having their backs against an unknown wilderness and desired the protection of Salem Towne. Virtually all of the afflicted lived on the Parris supporter side of the village. Likewise, most of those accused of witchcraft lived on the anti-Parris side of the village nearest Salem Towne five miles east. The hangings took place in Salem Towne, not Salem Village.

Why did Sarah use a map and draw an extended line through the meetinghouse and the middle of Salem Village? What did it show?

How was the list of names proof of a conspiracy between the two Parris factions of the village?

45 / 45   Although the awarding of the three sovereigns is creative license, the symbolic implications are exemplary in spirit to the actual recompense given the surviving families of Sarah's sisters in 1711 by the colony and the Province of Massachusetts. That part was aligned with history. The recompense absolved the three sisters and all other accused persons of any guilt. Money was also given to both the Nurse family and the Easty family in Rebecca and Mary's name in recompense.

45 / 45
(cont'd)

Just prior to this date, the covenant members of the living church of Salem Towne overturned Rebecca's excommunication, thus restoring her soul to God. At the same time, in the same church, Anne Putnam Sr. sought membership and was allowed in after apologizing to the congregation for her part in falsely accusing others of witchcraft.

Three gold sovereigns was worth about one dollar in colonial times – not a great deal of money. Why was Sarah so grateful to receive them?

46 / 19

The Epilogue takes no creative license except for the three sovereigns...

- END OF SERIES -

www.Salem-Witch-Trials.com

- SUPPLEMENTAL READING -

(ADULT: NON-FICTION)

"Salem Possessed: The Social Origins of Witchcraft":
Boyer, Paul and Nissenbaum, Stephen
1984, Paper back, Harvard University press

"The Devil in Massachusetts: A Modern Enquiry into the Salem Witch Trials":
Starkey, Marion L.
1969, Paperback, Doubleday

"Salem Witchcraft": (Vol. I & Vol. II)
Upham, Charles W.
1959, Ungar

"Witchcraft at Salem":
Hansen, Chadwick
1985, Paperback, Braziller

(JUVENILE: NON-FICTION)

"Witchcraft at Salem Village":
Jackson, Shirley

"The Story of the Salem Witch Trials":
Kent, Zachary
1986, Paperback, Children's Press

(*Note: with the exception of the Upham book, all of these publications are available in paperback. Fictitious works include the stage play, "Crucible," by Arthur Miller, which makes a nice study by comparison of fact versus fiction. There were also many conflicting accounts of the day by ministers and writers such as Robert Calef and the works of Increase Mather and his son Cotton Mather. Periodicals dealing with the production include; English Journal: Vol, 75; Number 6, October 1986. pg. 64 and American Magazine: Vol. 13; Number 2, May/June 1985. pg. 60)

**78 Spanish Moss Lane
The Henry Ford Plantation
Richmond Hill, GA 31324**

IN ASSOCIATION WITH:

1320 Braddock Place, Alexandria, VA 22314

www.Salem-Witch-Trials.com

NOTES

Made in the USA
Las Vegas, NV
02 September 2021